The Royal Baths and Pump Room
Royal [illegible]ington Spa

About 1820 showing the early Parish Church and the hump-backed bridge

This was easily the most important single building in the establishment of Leamington as a Spa. Even today it is a distinctive and well-known feature of the town. The Pump Room buildings have had quite a number of extensive alterations; inside and out, since their conception and yet they have until recently continued to perform their intended function. Up to 1997, as in the early days, they have been a most flourishing medical establishment, functioning at full capacity to provide physiotherapy and hydrotherapy treatments.

In the period just prior to 1810 it had become obvious that the town's existing Bath Houses; in spite of many improvements, could not cope with the ever increasing volume of visitors. Plans were therefore made to build a bathing establishment on a scale far surpassing anything yet attempted; that would excel, in fact, all that had been built in England! Certainly the scheme was of the greatest importance to Leamington. A syndicate was formed to provide the necessary funds that comprised Messrs. B. B. Greatheed, of Guy's Cliffe, Warwick; John

Pump Room and New baths 1815

Tomes, a rich banker; H. W. Tancred, of Warwick and Parkes, also of Warwick. From the beginning it was the intention of the planners to erect their splendid new Baths in the already growing New Town i.e. north of the River Leam and away from the humbler area of the Old Town.

As the centre of the New Town developed around the present Regent Street area, great efforts were made to discover a reliable source of saline water. After numerous failed borings, the plan to build a Pump Room at the very heart of the new Spa was regretfully abandoned. It was a bitter disappointment to the speculators that the only saline water supply on the north side of the river was discovered (1810) just a stone's throw from the Old Town. The spring was reached at a depth of 34 feet on the 65 acre farm owned by Mr. B. B. Greatheed (who, fortunately, happened to be a member of the syndicate!). This farm had been worked by Farmer Perkins who paid an annual rent of £70 but when the farm was sold it realised between £40,000 and £50,000 which was considered at the time to be a moderate price compared with other suitable building land in the New Town.

As the "North" well was so near to the River Leam it was rather isolated from all the new main buildings about to be erected on the new "Parade". It would mean that patrons of the Baths would need to make the journey down the long hill and, after their visit, make the tiring trip back. There was also another matter of a more unpleasant nature which no doubt displeased the syndicate. In the early days all the raw sewage from the New Town emptied into the River Leam just a few hundred yards from the North well. It was at least down-river but hardly down-wind! On a hot sultry summer day the cream of society strolling in the nearby Pump Room Gardens, would not favour the resultant aroma or the visual aspect of the river. When the gardens were actually in use there does not appear to be any record of complaints so perhaps the patrons were more accustomed to such circumstances than our modern antiseptic generation. There was actually a hint of concern, by the Pump Room owners, that the saline water may get polluted but it seems they were not very anxious about the possibility. From the discovery of the North well (1810) there was a delay of three years before building commenced. This was probably due to many prolonged trials carried out to make sure the supply of mineral water was adequate for the ambitious scheme.

The building was designed and built by C.S. Smith, of Warwick, and the plan was indeed both elegant and beautiful in it's simple, well-balanced layout. The total cost was nearly £30,000 and the town was justly proud when in July 1814, the "Pump Room Baths" were officially opened with well-deserved pomp. During the following year the title was changed to "The Royal Baths and Pump Room" (yet now, in 1999,the title we see over the colonnade is the "Royal Pump Room and Baths"). The complete design was not, in fact, carried out until 1819.

The Pump Room formed the main central feature. It was made of native stone and was over 100 feet in length and 30 feet high surrounded on three sides by a spacious colonnade; the roof being of a simple cottage style. The splendid Pump Room had an entrance at either end and beyond these extended the two wings 30 feet long and 20 feet high. These wings formed the entrances to the Public Baths that comprised 20 baths in all (17 hot and 3 cold) of which three were set aside for charitable purposes. Facilities were available from 7 a.m. to 3 p.m. daily (except during times of Divine Service). A local guide book (1830) gives us the following information:-

> The baths comprised hot, cold, tepid, vapour, plunging and shower baths, hot and cold douche (with a 30 ft. fall of water) for topical applications, and a chair bath; an excellent contrivance for conveying the invalid, on the

About 1820 showing the early Parish Church and the hump-backed bridge

About 1830 with Newbold Villa on the left and the early Parish Church in the distance

About 1840. View from the Mill including the Parish Church, Victoria Terrace and Victoria Bridge

undressing chair into the bath, in a most safe and easy manner. All these baths are spacious and well constructed, formed with Dutch tiles, and most of them furnished with convenient dressing rooms.

There was certainly no hint of "mixed bathing" in the early days, in fact proper steps were taken to ensure that bathers were spared the embarrassment of meeting the opposite sex. We are informed that "there are two divisions of baths, entirely separated, one for the use of the ladies and the other for gentlemen; the appropriate entrances are through the wings at either end of the building".

The recommended time for baths was in the evening and as a rule a course of bathing was combined with taking the waters. The Spa treatment was claimed to cure or relieve a huge number of disorders including "stiffness of the tendons", "rigidity of the joints", "the effects of gout and rheumatism" and "various paralytic conditions". One contemporary observer wrote to a friend:-

"are you given to warm bathing? If you are, here is a treat for you. What a delightful consciousness of existance it induces - what a delicious atmosphere it spreads about you - how completely it separates the man from his clothes.
The Pump Room itself is of large size, of lofty height and noble proportions (75 ft. long x 28 ft. high). The ornaments of the ceiling, the cornices, and, in fact, all the internal embellishments are chaste and simply elegant. It is lighted on one side by a range of seven windows, and, on the opposite side, by one large window of coloured glass: below which are two beautiful chimney pieces of Kilkenny marble. At the east end of the room, on an ornamental Derbyshire marble pedestal, stands the pump, having a basin in the centre, enclosed in a neat mahogany balustrade; here the Visitors drink the waters, receiving them from the pumpers (obliging damsels). Hours for taking the waters and promenading the Pump-Room are from 7 to 10 in the morning".

About 1840 with Euston Place on the right and the Lower Parade in the distance

About 1845 with Victoria Colonnade, Victoria Bridge and Bath Street

The 'season' for drinking the waters began in May and ended at the close of October. It was considered that the weather during this period would be good enough so that "early rising can be put in practice with safety to the invalid". Patients, such as frail young damsels, with particularly delicate constitutions and therefore unable to brave the elements in the morning, "frequently had the waters conveyed to them in such a vessel as a Florence Flask".

The Spa water is a mild laxative and that is really the only reason why the water was drunk. The following advice was given regarding the taking of the waters:-

> Patients should take preparatory steps in order to get the best results from the waters: using aperient (laxative) medicines and occasional local and general bleeding (blood-letting). The drink of saline water to be one pint, half a pint at 7 a.m., on an empty stomach, the second half pint about 20 minutes later. Frequency of taking the waters to be twice or thrice a week and a trial period of one month is advised.

Patients were warned that :-

> Indiscriminate use of large doses of the waters proves to be very hurtful to the constitution - causing, in particular, diarrhoea of the most troublesome nature.

(For drinking purposes it would appear that the Spa water was raised by a simple hand pump). Dr. A. B. Granville, a fashionable and eminent London doctor, wrote in his *Spas of England* (1841), quite a detailed description of the Spa of Leamington. His comments on this particular resort were in the main extremely critical and scornful - perhaps he had good cause - even so, it certainly seems there was an element of "sour grapes". Probably his opinions hastened the decline of Leamington as an inland Spa during the next 10 years? Regarding the Pump Room he said:-

> A respectable looking dame presides at the counter, she draws the water by that most objectionable of all modes, a pump, whose pipes descend into the depth of 34 ft. in the well containing the "saline water"; but not so deep in that twin-well which supplies the one charged with sulphureted hydrogen gas; those being the two sorts of mineral waters discovered on this spot.

His distaste of the waters was expressed as follows:

> The water, when cold, tastes unpleasantly saltish; when warmed, this taste is even more nauseous!

(This fact, however, may have had a greater attraction to patients who felt that if the medicine tasted nasty it must be all the more effective!)
Another writer tells us "when drawn from the pumps the waters are sparkling and transparent, and make a slightly buzzing noise, from the escape of the gaseous contents. The odour is slightly pungent.

G ranville remarks that the laxative effect of the water was slight and that, for some patients, a large quantity needed to be consumed. He observed, with horror, that some people were not afraid "to use a huge tumbler which I saw on the counter and the sight positively frightened me" (he obviously considered that such an excessive intake was an injurious practice). Describing the other type of spa water (charged with sulphureted hydrogen gas) he states, "It is a water having an exceedingly nauseous taste; and a most objectionable look besides, being of a dark yellowish green hue, with many floating particles in it".

Another writer's description was not much better "these waters smell somewhat like rotten eggs"!

Moncrieff's 1830 guide says :-

> An orchestra (rostrum) is placed in the centre of the pump-room, on the west side, where, in the morning, from 8 to 9 a.m. (the usual time of taking the waters), a well selected band attends regularly on week days - for the crowds of aristocratic patrons, as they quaffed their goblets at the fount before breakfast.

In contrast to other descriptions, Dr. Granville made the following chilly comment on the interior of the Pump Room:- "It has four naked walls, distempered over with deep peach blossom colour, having on one side high chimney pieces of painted wood and plasters similarly painted, to imitate Sienna marble; with a plain white-washed ceiling, from which hangs pendant an ordinary chandelier, serving to light up at night four casts of statues in different parts of the room".

In 1830 the charges were :-

Terms for drinking the waters	
One person the season	21/-
Two persons, same family	31/6
For a family	42/-
One person for a month	10/6
For a family for a month	21/-
Two persons, same family, for a month	15/-
One person for a week	3/6

Terms for bathing	
Warm bath	3/-
For a child	2/-
Cold bath	1/6

In all cases the addition of a gratuity to the attendant.

A local guide (1842) stated:-

> we can confidently assert the pump room is one of the most magnificent structures of the kind in the kingdom. The attendants there are attentive and clever in the performance of their duties; we may add to these recommendations also, that there is no place in the land where the experience is larger or the reputation more widely extended, as applicable to medical practitioners. When not in use, the warm baths are always kept and shown empty, and are either filled in the Visitor's presence, or while he is preparing to use them.

It is important to mention that the supply of saline water (for the several Bath Houses) in Leamington was plentiful and this great asset had a powerful influence on the fashionable world; turning the tide in favour of Leamington and away from it's more established rival Spa of Cheltenham. It was well known that Cheltenham suffered an acute shortage of the vital mineral waters - in a busy season there was only just sufficient water available for drinking purposes - and this meant that the local Baths there had to be content with the use of fresh water for bathing purposes.

Leamington naturally made the most of it's advantage and proudly stressed IT'S abundant supply and pointed out that "individual baths filled before your eyes" (to assure patients that they were

Situated in an annexe, the Spa water fountain was used by the public until 1997

not stepping into water already used by the previous bather!). An event in 1825 indicated the ample supply of saline water. A large fire broke out in the Bath Street area and, after a while, the firemen exhausted all the nearby fresh water springs so that, as a last resort, they connected their engines to a source of saline water at Abbott's Baths in Bath Street. The supply was so plentiful the fire was soon entirely subdued. Even the critical Dr. Granville had to grudgingly admit that there was no shortage of spa water at Leamington!

It is indicative of the importance and magnitude of the Pump Room project that one of Britain's most famous engineers was employed in the fitting out of the premises. He was William Murdock, known to many as the inventor of lighting by coal gas (1792). The historian Smiles stated that Murdock "was engaged in erecting an apparatus of his own invention for heating water for the baths and that while so employed a ponderous cast-iron plate fell upon his leg, above the ankle, and severely injured him. He remained a long time in Leamington and when it was thought safe to remove him, the Birmingham Canal Company kindly placed their excursion boat at his disposal, and he was conveyed safely homeward" (to Handsworth). With a note of pride, a local guide informed it's readers that "'the most judicious arrangements are made for expeditiously emptying and filling the baths and raising them to any required degree of heat.

At this time Murdock was employed by the world-famous firm of Boulton and Watt of the Soho Foundry, Birmingham. He was an outstanding engineer with a great capacity for inventiveness - he once invented and built a working model of a steam driven road carriage before any such vehicle existed. For 15 years he was James Watt's chief erector of his engines in Cornwall and his personal efforts greatly contributed to Watt's triumph in that county of tin and copper mines. Later Murdock worked closely with Boulton and Watt "in bringing to a state of perfection the condensing steam engine - the greatest lever of commerce, all the world over". The engineering work at the Pump Room included the installation of a 2 horse-power steam engine to pump up the saline water. James Bisset, in one of his flamboyant guide books of the period, wrote, "The beautiful engine could force up as many tons of the mineral fluid in a few hours, as would fairly float a British Man of War". Moncrieff (1830) described the pump as "a beautiful specimen of this astonishing invention"; while the *Illustrated London News* (1846) praised the machine as "being able to do hundredfold the work of the old well-windlass. (Some of the earlier Baths in the town used a single live horse to operate their pumps). The Industrial revolution had truly intruded into the genteel atmosphere of the new Spa!

Shortly after the opening of the Pump Room the land adjacent was laid out and enclosed as a garden for the exclusive use of patrons "to afford them pleasant promenades. An orchestra (rotunda) has been erected on the walks, where a military band is in attendance, in the evening during the summer, for the gratification of the subscribers as they walk around the gay and pleasing circular grounds" (it was not until 1889 that the Pump Room Gardens became public).

Dr. Granville stated "At Leamington, unquestionably, no dross of society or even ambiguous characters, will be found among those who assemble at the Pump Room for their health and the waters. The place is yet too choice and too costly to admit of any but the very tip-top of society. The elite of society congregate together at Leamington in countless numbers, determined to go thither and nowhere else. The elite comprise dukes and duchesses, marquesses, earls and barons, with their coronetted partners - not to mention the many Lady Augustas and Louisas, baronets and their spouses, besides military knights and their ladies. The Royal Pump Room was, for the majority, the rendezvous for those of fashion and rank - although very few actually go there to drink the waters".

As we have already stated, the presence of the Royal Pump Room & Baths was a key factor in the success of Leamington as a Spa. However, no history of this establishment would be complete without proper reference to Dr. Henry Jephson as he, without doubt, was the human instrument who put the Spa (and the Pump Room) well and truly "on the map". Jephson came first to Leamington in 1819 and, except for two short absences, spent the remaining 50 years of his life in the town. He was an eminent and vastly popular physician; full of energy and confidence, kind and gentle (when the need arose), warmly generous and extremely concerned, not only with all his patients but also in the welfare of the town. Jephson's "legend" spread far and wide and patients from all over England;

"Drinking the waters", 1874

About 1905. The building as modified 1861-63

even from other countries, flocked to the flourishing Spa for his treatment which comprised attendance at the Pump Room, diet and great amount of walking. The distinguished and much beloved doctor was indeed the "Star" of Leamington; in fact, to the cream of Society, Jephson WAS "Leamington".

Among his patients were Princess Victoria (later Queen), her mother the Duchess of Kent, George IV, Florence Nightingale (also her mother and sister) and W. E. Gladstone. Other notable visitors coming to the town for the waters (and no doubt, under Dr. Jephson's supervision) were the Duke & Duchess of Bedford, the Duke & Duchess of Gloucester, Princess Augusta and a host of other titled persons. These were the colourful figures of class and distinction that were seen partaking of the waters and/or socialising as they promenaded at the truly "Royal" Pump Room. The opening of this grand establishment proved to be the death knell for all the other Baths in town as, after a short while, they were put out of business due to lack of customers. Even so it's creation had placed Leamington on a level with the most fashionable health resorts in the kingdom.

At first the income paid was handsome but by 1848 the importance of Leamington as a spa began to decline and the future looked bleak. Consequently, the original syndicate broke up and the Pump Room and Baths became the sole property of the Hon. Charles Bertie Percy of Guy's Cliffe. Owing to the continued decline of the Pump Room and Baths, in 1860 he announced his intention to close the building and put it up for sale as a building plot. In May of that year the "Courier" newspaper alerted the people of Leamington to the great loss this would mean for the town and urged that a local syndicate should quickly be formed to acquire the premises. There was an immediate response to this appeal from a number of prominent residents including Dr. Jeaffreson, Mr. Summerfield, Mr. Matthew Wise and Mr. John Haddon. Several meetings were called during June for the towns people to support the syndicate and form the "Royal Leamington Spa Pump Room Association" in order to raise £8,000.

A year after the "Courier" first announced the Association (May 1861) it was dissolved because only £4,300 had been subscribed against the purchase price of £8,500. On July 13th 1861, the "Courier" announced that the project they had fostered had again been revived. A company to be known as "The Leamington Royal Pump Room Company Ltd" had been formed under the chairmanship of Dr. Henry Jephson together with a provisional committee of 41 influential townspeople. Following this activity, on September 5th 1861 a meeting of the Company was held when it was announced that the whole of the purchase price had been raised and was paid to the Hon Bertie Percy. The Company took possession during October 1861. From this date and to the end of 1863, large-scale improvements were carried out under the direction of the architect J. Cundall. The Company had the original cottage-style roof replaced and on the front elevation was added a tower at the north end, a central pediment, balustrade, cornice and stucco facing. The windows were also altered. Inside, there were new baths, a public swimming pool (the first in the building later becoming the "Ladies" pool and finally the therapeutic pool) and a Turkish bath. Mr. J.H. Clarke of Warwick carried out the work while Mr. James Marriott of Coventry completed other portions of the interior.

In spite of all the renovations and improvements the Baths still failed to become a financial success and in 1868 were sold to the Local Board of Health for £15,000.

During 1869 the fencing on the Parade frontage was removed from the "Pump Room Gardens" and a broad footpath was laid. Then, in 1875, the Linden Avenue was thrown open to the general public and finally, in 1889, a resolution was approved that the "Pump Room Gardens" should also be opened to the public free of charge.

Leamington Corporation was formed in 1875 and the Borough Council from then carried out the functions of the existing Local Board of Health including control of the Pump Rooms. In 1885 the Pump Room Committee borrowed £4,000 to pay for a complete renovation of the Baths including the installation of some new ones by Messrs. Jenkins and Son of Leamington. These alterations were planned by Mr. W. de Normanville, Borough Surveyor and the work was finished by 1887. The Speaker of the House of Commons, Mr. Arthur Wellesley Peel, performed the opening ceremony.

A short time later the large, second swimming pool, designed by Mr. W. de Normanville, was built at a cost of £2,500 and opened in 1890 by John Fell, Mayor (the pool closed to the public on the 27th June 1990). The Pump Room Annexe was added as a south wing in 1910 and in 1926 an ambitious programme of rebuilding, renovations and reorganisation was embarked upon. At a cost of

About 1930. The large public swimming pool (1890). Now the new home of the public library

£15,000 the work was carried out under the guidance of Alderman K.R. England, the then chairman of the Pump Room Committee.

Plans were approved in December 1950 for the removal of the tower and centre pediment on the front elevation. Alterations were made to the roof, and the balustrade, cornice and stucco facing removed; the existing brickwork being replaced in ashlar veneer. The work was completed in 1953.

Major improvements to the large swimming pool commenced in December 1955 and on October 12th 1956 the pool was re-opened.

1981. The therapeutic pool, established about 1950. Originally was the small public swimming pool (1863); later ladies pool. Now new home of the Art Gallery

About 1910. The Assembly Room with the spa water fountain and serving counter on the right.

About 1925. The annexe with the spa water fountain and serving counter on the left.

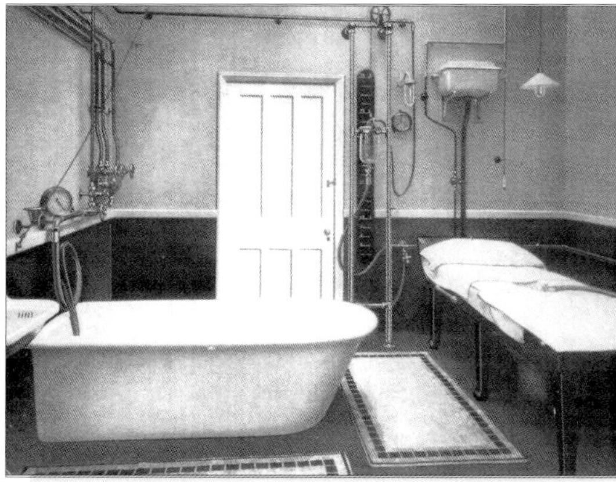

About 1925. The Plombieres Department; one of the many medical baths

Leamington Corporation owned the Pump Room up to 1974 when the Warwick District Council took over. By the late 1980's it was decided that the building was again in need of expensive restoration work. Warwick District Council closed down the medical department in December 1990 and consequently the National Health Service physiotherapy unit began to provide treatment early in 1991 at the Warneford Hospital. However, this was not for long as the hospital closed down at the end of October 1993 and at the same time the unit (about 10 strong) returned to the Pump Room on the 26th October. They finally moved to a Portocabin in Court Street in 1997.

About 1986 two private consortia proposed plans for the refurbishment of the Pump Rooms but both were unable to obtain necessary funds and the schemes failed. Then, between 1987 and 1996 Warwick District Council invited local architects and other bodies to present their own plans for the revitalisation

About 1920. Assembly Room in use as a Tea Room

of the Pump Rooms but not one of the four proposals received were to be adopted. During May 1996, the Warwick District Council (which owns the property), in collaboration with Warwick County Council, produced proposals using public money to relocate Leamington's Art Gallery, Museum and Library to the Pump Rooms. During the following months the scheme was further developed to include the refurbishment of the Assembly Room within the Pump Rooms and provision for the Tourist Information Centre and Cafeteria so creating a major cultural and tourist attraction.

About 1960. Lesley Clay Trio in the Tea Room

The whole pump room complex closed to the public in October, 1997 and in the following month work began to implement the agreed final proposals of 1996.